the
parenting
teenagers
course

for those parenting
11 to 18-year-olds

> Guest Manual

Contents

This manual is designed to be used on The Parenting Teenagers Course with the DVDs or live talks. See page 78 for more information on how to join or run a course.

Acknowledgements

We are very grateful indeed to the following people for their help and encouragement in the creation of The Parenting Teenagers Course:

Rob Parsons, for his inspiration, stories and illustrations in his books and talks.

Ross Campbell, for the insights in his books, especially on managing anger.

Gary Chapman, for the help that his concept of the five love languages has been to us and many other parents.

Nicky and Sila Lee

The authors and publisher gratefully acknowledge permission to reproduce copyright material in this book. Every effort has been made to trace and contact copyright holders. If there are any inadvertent omissions we apologise to those concerned and will ensure that a suitable acknowledgment is made in all future editions.

The exercise (p. 15) is adapted from Walt Mueller, *Understanding Today's Youth Culture*, Tyndale House Publishers, 1994 and reproduced by permission of the author.

The table (p. 23) is adapted from Tim Smith, *Almost Cool*, Moody Publishers, 1997 and is reproduced by permission of the publisher.

The diagram (p. 32) is from Sue Palmer, *Toxic Childhood*, Orion Books, 2006 and reproduced by permission of the publisher.

The SMART rules for staying safe online (p. 63) are copyright © Childnet International 2002–2011 and are reproduced with permission. **childnet.com**

The exercise 'Facing Challenges' (p.70–72) is adapted from Michael and Terri Quinn, *What Can a Parent Do?*, Family Caring Trust, 1986 and reproduced by permission.

Keeping the End in Mind

Part 1 Understanding the transition

Aim of the course

- to strengthen your relationship(s) with your teenager(s)

Content of the course

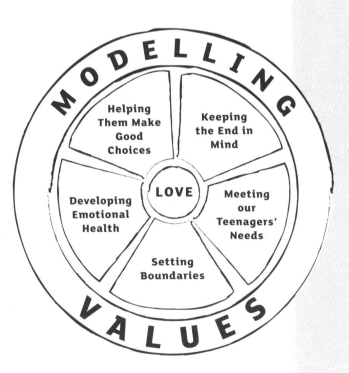

Principles of the course

- unhelpful to make comparisons: each family is unique and each parent has their own parenting style
- broad principles for parenting teenagers
- value of discussions with other parents

Adapting for this new stage of parenting

1. Make adjustments

- the teenage years are a time of transition
- they're changing and we need to change the way we parent them
- the onset of puberty
- the effects of new hormones
- teenagers need understanding and acceptance as well as guidance and boundaries

2. Understand the pressures

- pressures on teenagers:
  - consumer society
  - expectations to achieve
  - desire to conform to their peer group
- pressures on parents of teenagers:
  - speed of life
  - emotional energy required

3. Remember our long-term aim

- maintaining and building our relationship with our teenagers
- helping them grow into mature, responsible adults
- developing their character and helping them to learn good values

Building character

What are the characteristics you hope your teenager(s) will develop eventually?
Write some of them down.
(eg: honesty, self-control, respect for authority, faithfulness, responsibility)

1. _____

2. _____

3. _____

4. _____

How could you help them to develop these characteristics?

1. _____

2. _____

3. _____

4. _____

Discuss what you have put down with one or two others.

For 10-week course only

Small group discussion

1. What do you think are the main pressures on your teenagers(s) at the moment?

_____

_____

2. What are the main pressures on you?

_____

_____

3. What has helped to build your relationship with your teenager(s)?

_____

_____

4. How are you helping your teenager(s) to develop one of the characteristics you wrote in the exercise above?

_____

_____

Homework – complete **Exercise 1** on page 15

Part 2 Building strong relationships

The role of the family

- the family continues to be important for teenagers
- our home is an expression of our family life

1. Home as a place of safety and acceptance

- our family can be a shelter from the different storms our teenagers will face: disappointment, failure, rejection
- when they are hurt, they need our comfort and consolation
- we can demonstrate this practically by allowing them to talk and by listening to them
- effective communication with teens requires time
- discussing and debating with teenagers is more effective than lecturing and judging them

2. Home as the place to learn good values

- teenagers learn more from what they see than from what we tell them to do
- learning to be honest, generous and hospitable; learning to handle anger, to resolve conflict, to apologise and to forgive
- 'like father like son'; 'like mother like daughter' - our teenagers will learn more from us than from anyone else, if we're there for them

3. Home as a place of fun

- as parents we may need to lighten up
- teenagers want to be where the fun is
- can they bring their friends home? Consider creating some teenage-friendly space in your house
- have relaxed family mealtimes
- laugh together
- the value of family holidays

Glynis Good *
British Psychological Society *
Catherine.

(Mealtimes)

↓
good food
↓
relaxation
↓
debate
↓
contribute.

4. Home as the place to learn about relationships

- teenagers learn to relate through observing adult relationships
- if parenting together, invest in your relationship (consider doing The Marriage Course)
- if parenting on your own, build the best relationship you can with the other parent (if they are around)
- nurture other adult friendships
- mealtimes together – teenagers learn to talk, listen, debate issues and respect others' views
- regular family time – having fun together as a family helps build relationships between parents and children and between siblings (consider having a weekly 'family night')

For 5-week course only
Small group discussion

1. What do you think are the main pressures on your teenager(s) at the moment?

_____

_____

2. What are the main pressures on you?

_____

_____

3. How could you help to support your teenager(s)?

_____

_____

4. Do you have regular family time?

_____

_____

5. What have been the most successful holidays you have had as a family?

_____

_____

Homework – complete **Exercises 1** and **2** on pages 15–17

Small group discussion

1. How could you help to support your teenager(s)?

_____

_____

2. What values are you seeking to pass on?

_____

_____

3. What changes would you like to make to your family life/your house?

_____

_____

4. Do you have regular family time daily/weekly?

_____

_____

5. What have been the most successful holidays you have had as a family?

_____

_____

Homework – complete **Exercise 2** on page 16–17

Homework

Exercise 1 (to discuss with your teenager(s))

Ask your teenager(s) which of the following are most important to them:

1. Parents who don't argue in front of them.

2. Parents who treat each member of the family the same.

3. Parents who are honest.

4. Parents who are tolerant of others.

5. Parents who welcome their friends into their home.

6. Parents who build a sense of family identity.

7. Parents who answer their questions.

8. Parents who impose sanctions when needed but not in front of others, especially their friends.

9. Parents who concentrate on good points instead of weaknesses.

10 Parents who are consistent.

11. Parents who don't shout at them.

12. Parents who don't pressurise them.

13. Parents who listen to them.

14. Parents who spend time with them.

Adapted from Walt Mueller, *Understanding Today's Youth Culture*

Exercise 2

How much time do you spend (on average) with your teenager(s)?

1. Do you see them on a weekday in the morning? YES/NO

   If so, for how long? _____

2. Do you see them on a weekday in the evening? YES/NO

   If so, for how long? _____

3. Do you spend time with them at a weekend? YES/NO

   If so, for how long on a Saturday? _____

   If so, for how long on a Sunday? _____

4. Do you spend time together as a family? YES/NO

   If so, how often? _____

   For how long? _____

5. Do you spend time with each child on his or her own? YES/NO

   If so, how often? _____

   For how long? _____

Exercise 2 (continued)

6. Write down changes, if any, that you would like to make to your routine.

Weekdays:

_____

_____

_____

Weekends:

_____

_____

_____

2
Meeting our
Teenagers' Needs

Review

Session 1 – Keeping the End in Mind

- helping our teenager(s) towards maturity and independence
- our home needs to be:
  - a place of safety
  - a place of learning values for life
  - a place of fun
  - a place of learning to build relationships
- building a healthy family life
  - family meals
  - family time (having fun together)
  - family holidays

Discuss

- What was most relevant for you from Session 1?

- Have you organised any 'family time' since then?

Part 1 The five love languages

Building our teenagers' confidence

- our teenagers' greatest need is to feel loved and accepted during this enormous transition in their lives – a time of:
  - self-discovery
  - pushing for independence
  - much self-questioning
  - peer pressure

loveable person

uniquely valued
uniquely precious

- they can experience a lot of self-doubt and feel awkward and unlovable
- confidence rests on:
  - security (knowing they are loved)
  - self-worth (knowing they are of value)
  - significance (knowing there is a purpose to their lives)
- seek to keep their 'emotional tank' full of love:
  - their behaviour acts like the gauge to show how full of love they feel
- knowing that they are loved and accepted enables them in the long-term:
  - to resist peer pressure when they need to
  - to make good choices
  - to build close relationships

Discovering how our teenagers feel loved

- discover the primary way each teenager feels loved, whether it's through:
  - time
  - words
  - touch
  - presents
  - actions
  (see Gary Chapman, *The Five Love Languages of Teenagers*)
- importance of a particular love language may have changed as a child has grown older

1. One-to-one time

- the importance of giving our teenagers our undivided attention
- doing something with them – it doesn't have to be expensive
- ask them what they enjoy doing
- don't set the bar too high – seize opportunities, eg: go out for a pizza, walk the dog together, play or watch sport, go to the cinema or a concert
- consider spending a more extended period of time with each child once a year

2. Affirming words

- the words we speak to our teenagers can stay with them for the rest of their lives
- tell them of your love and pride in them
- affirm them (not just when they please you; not just for their achievements)
- affirm their looks
- aim at five positive comments for every one negative comment
- find things for which to praise them
- loving words build confidence and affect their attitudes
- loving words can be spoken and written

3. Affectionate touch

- teenagers can be embarrassed by physical affection yet also long for it
- avoid embarrassing them
- find appropriate moments and ways to maintain physical contact if they're feeling self-conscious

4. Thoughtful presents

- a way of showing our unconditional love – not only dependent on their behaviour or performance
- to mark birthdays, Christmas/other festivals
- use presents to celebrate achievements or to bring consolation when they're struggling
- can be small but make big impact
- find out what's special for each child

5. Kind actions

- see the regular kind actions you do on their behalf as a way of showing them your love
- look for opportunities to do something extra for them
- be careful not to rescue them – otherwise they won't learn from their mistakes

- give teenagers increasing responsibility
  – don't do everything for them
- remind them to express gratitude for what
  we or others do for them

For 5- and 10-week courses
Exercise

Ranking the love languages

One-to-one time – Affirming words – Affectionate touch – Thoughtful presents – Kind actions

1. What is the relative importance of these five ways of expressing love for yourself and for your teenager(s)/pre-teen(s)? Try to rank them in order of priority:

Yourself:

1. _____

2. _____

3. _____

4. _____

5. _____

Child:

1. _____

2. _____

3. _____

4. _____

5. _____

Child (if relevant):

1. _____

2. _____

3. _____

4. _____

5. _____

Child (if relevant):

1. _____

2. _____

3. _____

4. _____

5. _____

(Do a similar list for any additional children)

Please turn over ⇨

Exercise (continued)

2. How could these lists be helpful in your parenting over the coming week?

_____

_____

Discuss what you have put down with one or two others.

For 10-week course only
Small group discussion

1. Which of the five ways of expressing love was most important for you during your upbringing?

_____

_____

2. Can you remember a particular example of your parent(s) showing love to you in this way?

_____

_____

3. How did it make you feel?

_____

4. Which of the five expressions of love do you find it hardest to show to your children?

_____

Homework – complete **Exercise 1** on pages 28–9

Part 2 Effective communication

Adapting our approach

- communication not always easy through the teenage years
- learning curve for most parents
- adults and teenagers tend to communicate in different ways

The way many adults tend to communicate	The way most teenagers tend to communicate
By using reason, logic, one topic at a time	Stream of consciousness, easily switching between topics
To solve problems, get results, change behaviour	By talking at length without looking for solutions
By lecturing or moralising, at times getting heavy and intense	Like to leave things open-ended; don't need to have a 'point'; enjoy talking for its own sake
Interrogation style: *'Have you ... ?'*, *'Are you ... ?'*, *'Aren't you ...?'* etc	Open up when we least expect it and usually not to order
Often drawing on much experience to support arguments; holding a firm viewpoint	Often drawing on limited experience to make their point; exploring options
Pushing to know the whole situation, to learn all the details	Less focused; more easily distracted; shorter attention-span
Generally in a hurry. Have high expectations of what can be achieved in a short amount to time	Can't rush them. They are on their own timetable – often it's very slow

Adapted from Tim Smith, *Almost Cool*

- if we allow them to tell us what they find difficult about how we communicate with them, they are more likely to listen to us when we need to tell them what we find difficult about how they communicate with us
- understand that sometimes teenagers like to be contrary. (If we get heavy and intense they will probably react strongly just to give us a hard time)
- give them space. Respect their privacy. Don't try to control every aspect of their lives. Don't expect them to tell you everything

Communicating effectively with teenagers

1. Be available

- demonstrating we're available and ready to listen helps our teenagers open up
- take opportunities for significant conversations when they come up – not always at the most convenient moments for us!
- set aside regular time to talk

2. Learn to listen

- treat them like young adults (not children). Listen carefully to their views and feelings
- 'Effective communication requires that parents learn to speak with their teenager rather than at their teenager ...' Gary Chapman, *The Five Love Languages of Teenagers*
- engage in discussion and be prepared to debate the issues rather than repeating simplistic slogans such as 'You're too young to have a boyfriend', 'Drugs are dangerous'

3. Give your full attention

- recognise the important moments to listen and give your full attention
- don't try to listen to your teenager while doing something else at the same time

- maintain eye contact; observe your teenager's body language

4. Show an interest in the world of your teenager(s)

- ask questions about their interests and listen to their answers
- treat them as unique individuals with their own points of view and personal tastes

5. Listen for feelings

- allow them to express negative emotions
- don't rush in with solutions straightaway

6. Try to avoid interrupting

- the average person listens for only seventeen seconds
- resist the desire to be defensive or to butt in and correct

7. Reflect back what they have said

- say back to them what you think they are trying to express, particularly their feelings
- use some of their own words and phrases

8. Respond appropriately

- give guidance and reassurance
- they are likely to remember our words for years to come

9. Take a long-term view

- sometimes any meaningful communication with teenagers can be a big struggle
- difficulties are usually the result of a phase they're going through
- try to create the conditions for conversation to become easier, eg: at mealtimes; spending time with them doing what they enjoy; using their love language
- if worried, seek professional help and/or medical support

For 5- and 10-week courses
Exercise

Reflecting back

Spend a few minutes practising 'reflecting back' in pairs:

One person is a teenager with an issue to discuss. The other is the parent. The 'teenager' tells the 'parent' something he/she is worried about, *eg: disappointed not to be in a sports team or a play at school; struggling with schoolwork; worried about a friendship; anxious about what to say if offered drugs at a party.*

The 'parent' reflects back the issue, particularly the feelings that have been expressed. The 'teenager' talks a bit more about the situation and the 'parent' keeps reflecting back. Keep the conversation going for a minute or two and then swap roles.

For 5-week course only
Small group discussion

1. In the exercise on 'reflecting back', how did it feel to be listened to?

_____

_____

2. Which of the points on listening is most important/most difficult for you?

_____

_____

3. When have you had your best conversations with your teenagers/pre-teens?

_____

_____

4. Which of the five ways of expressing love was most important for you when you were a teenager?

_____

_____

5. Can you remember a particular example of your parent(s) showing love to you in this way? How did it make you feel?

_____

_____

6. Which of the five expressions of love do you find it hardest to show to your teenager(s)?

_____

_____

Homework – complete **Exercises 1** and **2** on pages 28–30

For 10-week course only
Small group discussion

1. In the exercise on 'reflecting back', how did it feel to be listened to?

_____

_____

2. How easy or difficult is it for you to communicate with your teenager(s)/ pre-teen(s) currently?

_____

_____

Please turn over ▷

Small group discussion (continued)

3. What are the principal interests that they enjoy talking about?

_____

_____

4. Which of the points on listening is most important/most difficult for you?

_____

_____

5.When have you had your best conversations with your teenager(s)/pre-teen(s)?

_____

_____

Homework – complete **Exercise 2** on page 29–30

Homework 🖋

Exercise 1

Speaking affirming words

Write down five positive qualities of each of your children.

Child's name: _____	Child's name: _____
1. _____	1. _____
2. _____	2. _____
3. _____	3. _____

4. _____   4. _____

5. _____   5. _____

Child's name: _____   Child's name: _____

1. _____   1. _____

2. _____   2. _____

3. _____   3. _____

4. _____   4. _____

5. _____   5. _____

Share what you have written with someone else.
Find a good moment to share them with your teenager(s)/pre-teen(s).

Exercise 2

Planning one-to-one time

1. Write a list of the interests of your child(ren):

Child's name: _____   Child's name: _____

1. _____   1. _____

2. _____   2. _____

3. _____   3. _____

4. _____   4. _____

5. _____   5. _____

Please turn over ⇨

Exercise 2 (continued)

Child's name: _____   Child's name: _____

1. _____   1. _____

2. _____   2. _____

3. _____   3. _____

4. _____   4. _____

5. _____   5. _____

2. What could you do during one-to-one time with each child that would help to build your relationship? Then write down when you could do this activity with them.

Child's name: _____   Child's name: _____

Activity _____   Activity _____

When _____   When _____

Child's name: _____   Child's name: _____

Activity _____   Activity _____

When _____   When _____

Setting Boundaries

Review

Session 1 – Keeping the End in Mind

- helping our teenager(s) towards maturity and independence
- making our home a place of safety, of learning values for life, of fun and of learning to build relationships
- building a healthy family life through family meals, family time (having fun together) and family holidays

Session 2 – Meeting our Teenagers' Needs

- importance of making our teenagers feel loved and accepted
- five ways of showing love through:
  - quality (one-to-one) time
  - affirming words
  - affectionate touch
  - thoughtful presents
  - kind actions
- one or more of these 'love languages' will be particularly important for each teenager to feel loved and to keep their 'emotional tank' full
- adapting our style of communication with our teenagers
- importance of listening
- listening involves:
  - being available
  - giving our full attention

– showing an interest in their world
– listening for feelings
– not interrupting
– reflecting back
– responding appropriately

Discuss:

- Have you tried using any of the five 'love languages' this week?
  If so, what was the effect?

- Have any of the points on listening made a difference in your relationship
  with your teenager(s)?

Part 1 Letting go gradually

Introduction

'Parents, do not exasperate your children; instead, bring them up in the training and instruction of the Lord.'

Ephesians 6:4
The Bible

- aim for 'authoritative' style of parenting, rather than an indulgent, neglectful or authoritarian style
- combination of warmth and firmness
- setting boundaries in the context of love

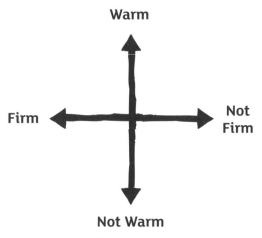

Source: Sue Palmer, *Toxic Childhood*

- we can't control our teenagers as we could when they were younger
- the culture they are growing up in is probably different to the one we grew up in
- change in attitudes towards authority today
- many parents are uncertain about setting boundaries or exercising authority
- boundaries remain important for teenagers
  - for their safety and welfare
  - for our family life
  - for their growth towards maturity
  - teenagers want limits
- setting boundaries with teenagers is hard
  - often no one, right, easy answer
  - we have to give them increasing freedom
  - we will make mistakes as parents
  - we can easily feel a failure, guilty, fearful
  - parental self-questioning is common, but, rather than seeing yourself on a tightrope, there's a broad path on which you can work out your own style
  - every teenager is different – much harder to set boundaries with some than with others
  - aim at being neither too strict nor too lenient
  - consistency is key

How to set boundaries with teenagers

1. Remember we're on the same side

- we're helping our teenagers on their journey to maturity
- see their desire for increasing independence as normal and healthy
- needs to be gradual handover of control
- no fixed timetable – teenagers mature at different speeds

2. Move from external to internal boundaries

- moving from parent control to self-control
- don't be too restrictive – allow them to learn from their own mistakes

3. Trust builds trustworthiness

- give them increasing responsibility so they learn to be responsible

4. Give increasing space

- start stricter and then increase their freedom as they show responsibility

> 'This ... moving from restrictiveness to privilege ... is not easy, for it takes courage and determination to make your teenager's privileges strictly dependent upon his or her ability to control his or her own behaviour. It takes strength to stand against the pressure for unearned concessions, not only from your teenager, but from other teenagers, other parents, and even society.'
>
> **Dr Ross Campbell,** *How to Really Love Your Teenager*

- giving too much freedom and having to backtrack means we're moving in the wrong direction

5. Allow them to make their own decisions

- let them have as much practice as possible over issues that will not jeopardise their future
- give them freedom to make choices in areas where they can express their individual preferences, eg: choice of clothes, room decoration, hairstyle, how they spend their pocket money/allowance

For 5- and 10-week courses
Exercise

Exercising authority

1. Do any of the following reasons make you reluctant to set boundaries with your teenager(s)?

   - Being fearful of your teenager's reaction ☐

   - Being afraid your teenager won't like you ☐

   - Feeling out of touch with their world ☐

   - Reacting against your own over-strict upbringing ☐

   - Thinking it won't make any difference ☐

   - Believing teenagers need complete freedom ☐

   - Your own circumstances ☐

   Other reasons

   _____

   _____

2. Do any of the following reasons make you reluctant to give your teenager(s) increasing freedom?

   - Wanting to stay in control of their lives ☐

   - Being afraid that they will make mistakes ☐

   - Trying to control who they spend their time with ☐

   - Not liking their individual preferences ☐

   - Fear of what other adults will think ☐

   - Wanting to know what they're doing at all times ☐

   - Thinking they will never be responsible enough ☐

   Other reasons

   _____

Discuss what you have put down with one or two others.

Small group discussion

1. What is hardest for you in setting boundaries with your teenager(s)?

_____

_____

2. Are there areas where you're giving them too much freedom?

_____

_____

3. Are there areas where you're being too restrictive?

_____

_____

4. What has helped you in this process of letting go gradually?

_____

_____

5. What decisions are you allowing them to make for themselves?

_____

_____

Homework – complete **Exercise 1** on pages 41–42

Part 2 Encouraging responsibility

How to help our teenagers move towards independence

- making our expectations clear
- giving them increasing responsibility, eg: to get up in the morning; to get ready for school; to take the books or sports equipment they need
- allowing them to bear the consequences of their own mistakes
- moving gradually from 'controller' to 'consultant'

'Parents face two options. We can keep using the same patterns we used when they were young (and frustrate ourselves to death), or we can realise that our methods must change as our kids develop ... As hard as it is, our role must move from controller to consultant. What do consultants do? They ask questions, offer opinions, share experiences, present options and forecast outcomes. Ultimately, however, they step back and allow the client to make decisions. Consultants understand what they can and cannot do for their client, and as a result the client owns the process as well as the results.'

Daniel Hahn in Tim Smith, *Almost Cool*

1. Don't nag

- nagging causes teenagers to tune out and switch off
- it sometimes makes them do the opposite of what we're saying

2. Make as few rules as possible

- say 'no' to the things that really matter and 'yes' to everything else
- decide on your own non-negotiables
  – resist being swayed by what others will think

- whenever possible agree rules with other parent and present a united front

3. Be sure you can explain the limits.

- teenagers need explanations for boundaries

> 'What causes adolescents to rebel is not the assertion of authority but the arbitrary use of power, with little explanation of the rules, and no involvement in decision making.'
>
> **Laurence Steinberg in Gary Chapman,**
> *The Five Love Languages of Teenagers*

4. Be prepared to negotiate

- discuss the boundaries with your teenager(s)
- be willing to listen – value their opinion
- be prepared to change your mind and make compromises
- be firm with important boundaries

5. Work out appropriate consequences

- impose a consequence when a rule is broken or trust has been abused
- make the sanction neither too lenient nor too harsh
- take time to consider what will teach them responsibility
- sometimes experiencing the natural consequence of their behaviour is most effective for them to learn – don't always rescue them
- sometimes knowing our disappointment is enough of a consequence to change their behaviour

Conclusion

- the alarm clock tip
- keep the end in mind

Small group discussion

1. How have you allowed your teenager(s) to grow in independence?
   What have you made them take responsibility for?

_____

_____

2. Can you think of a boundary you have negotiated with your teenager(s)?
   What was the result?

_____

_____

3. Have you had to become stricter over an issue? What was the result?

_____

_____

4. What consequences for wrong behaviour have you found to be effective?

_____

_____

5. Have you given them the opportunity to face challenges/pursue interests/
   explore/go on adventures? If so, what benefits have you seen for them to grow
   in responsibility?

_____

_____

Homework – complete **Exercises 1** and **2** on pages 41–43

For 10-week course only

Small group discussion

1. How have you allowed your teenager(s) to grow in independence? What have you made them take responsibility for?

_____

_____

2. Can you think of a boundary you have negotiated with your teenager(s)? What was the result?

_____

_____

3. Have you had to become stricter over an issue? What was the result?

_____

_____

4. What consequences for wrong behaviour have you found to be effective?

_____

_____

5. Have you given them the opportunity to face challenges/pursue interests/ explore/go on adventures? If so, what benefits have you seen for them to grow in responsibility?

_____

_____

Homework – complete **Exercise 2** on pages 42–43

Homework 🖊

Exercise 1

Recognising the important issues

Do the following exercise to see if you are expending most energy on the most important issues.

In **Column I**, put 1, 2, or 3 against each statement according to its comparative importance for you. (*1s = most important issues; 2s = less important; 3s = least important*)

In **Column II**, put 1, 2, or 3 against each statement according to how much time and emotional energy you expend on this aspect of your teenager's behaviour. (*1s = most time and energy; 2s = less time and energy; 3s = least time and energy*)

Are the numbers against each statement in your two columns the same as each other? If not, ask yourself which issues really are the most important for you in setting boundaries with your teenager(s). Be honest!

	I Importance of issue	II Amount of parental time and energy
1. Teenager's ability to be self-controlled		
2. A tidy room		
3. Top grade in all exams		
4. Mobile phone bill		
5. Being polite towards and considerate of others		
6. Being well-dressed (by your standards)		
7. Having friends with positive values		
8. Being responsible with alcohol and drugs		
9. Getting into the top team/playing in the school concert		
10. Piercing any/every part of his/her body		
11. Displaying loyalty in his/her friendships		
12. Getting into the school/college/ university of his/her choice		
13. Relating responsibly towards the opposite sex		
14. Showing generosity towards siblings and friends		

Please turn over ⇨

Exercise 1 (continued)

	I Importance of issue	II Amount of parental time and energy
15. Getting a tattoo		
16. Always doing his/her homework on time		
17. Honesty		
18. Having a hairstyle you like		
19. Growing in his/her relationship with God		
20. Contributing to the harmonious running of the home		

Exercise 2

Negotiating boundaries

Write down up to five 'non-negotiable' boundaries, *eg: your rules about drugs, honesty, homework, sexual behaviour*

1. _____

2. _____

3. _____

4. _____

5. _____

Exercise 2 (continued)

Write down up to five 'negotiable' boundaries, *eg: bedtime, parties, time on social networking sites, TV*

1. _____

2. _____

3. _____

4. _____

5. _____

Discuss your lists with your teenager(s)/pre-teen(s). Explain to them why each boundary is 'non-negotiable' or 'negotiable' and then listen carefully to their thoughts.

Negotiate an agreement on one of the 'negotiable' boundaries, including the consequence if they fail to keep to your agreement. Be prepared to make compromises.

4

Developing
Emotional Health

Review

Session 1 – Keeping the End in Mind

- helping our teenager(s) towards maturity and independence
- making our home a place of safety, of learning values for life, of fun and of learning to build relationships
- building a healthy family life through family meals, family time (having fun together) and family holidays

Session 2 – Meeting our Teenagers' Needs

- showing our teenager(s) love through (one-to-one) time, affirming words, affectionate touch, thoughtful presents and kind actions
- asking ourselves which 'love languages' make each teenager feel loved and keep their 'emotional tank' full
- remembering the importance of listening

Session 3 – Setting Boundaries

- remember we're on the same side
- let them go gradually
- give increasing independence
- as they mature, move from controller to consultant
- don't nag
- make as few rules as possible

- be willing to negotiate
- be firm with important boundaries
- work out effective sanctions if trust is broken or a boundary crossed

---

Discuss

- What boundaries have you had to impose this week?

- What were the results?

Part 1 Handling anger (ours and theirs)

Introduction

- the teenage years are often an emotionally stormy time
- parents have to learn to handle their own emotions
- we need to help our teenagers handle theirs, including:
  - learning to control anger
  - knowing how to resolve conflict
  - dealing with stress
- importance of reading each teenager's temperament

Understanding anger

- anger not wrong in itself
- our natural response to being upset
- anger can be expressed through words and/or behaviour
- we all need to learn to control and manage our anger constructively
- generally takes children at least 18 years to learn to express anger in a mature way

- inappropriate reactions to anger
  - uncontrolled anger is destructive ('rhino' behaviour)
  - unexpressed/suppressed anger is harmful ('hedgehog' behaviour)

'Rhino' behaviour	'Hedgehog' behaviour
Being aggressive	Burying anger
Shouting and screaming	Trying to ignore our feelings
Saying things we later regret	Becoming sarcastic
Losing control	Withdrawing behind an impenetrable wall
Lashing out and accusing	Becoming cold and clinical
Blaming everyone else	Feeling nervous or fearful
Becoming explosive or irritable	Wanting to run away and hide
Becoming controlling and bossy	Getting depressed

- 'displaced' anger – taking out our anger on someone else, sometimes years later
- anger must be dealt with at its source
- importance of choosing to forgive those who have hurt us, whether recently or a long time ago
- anger has a God-given purpose, but only for a short time

'Do not let the sun go down while you are still angry.'

Ephesians 4:26, The Bible

Managing our own anger effectively

1. Don't overreact

- recognise what causes you to overreact
- consider HALT (Are you Hungry, Anxious, Lonely or Tired?)
- find ways to help you press the 'pause button'

2. Don't be hurtful

- don't label your teenager
- label their action/their behaviour as wrong rather than attacking their character
- give them the opportunity and the belief that they can change

3. Don't withdraw

- don't avoid every disagreement
- don't become passive or switch off when there is conflict or an issue that needs to be addressed
- confront others when necessary and express your feelings

Helping our teenagers to use anger productively

- aim at encouraging neither aggression (rhino behaviour) nor suppression (hedgehog behaviour) but the expression of the cause of their anger
- don't expect too much too soon – it's a slow process of learning to express anger appropriately
- resist shutting them down when they express anger immaturely
- try not to respond to anger with anger
- teenagers often express anger through irritating behaviour ('passive aggressive' behaviour)
- allow them to verbalise their anger
- help them in this process of learning to express anger in a controlled way
- make your home a safe place to express negative feelings including grief and disappointment
- find opportunities to discuss with them appropriate and inappropriate expressions of anger

Expressions of anger

Look at the table for 'rhino' and 'hedgehog' behaviour.
Identify for yourself and your teenager(s) where each of you comes on the line
between rhino/hedgehog tendencies when angry. Then discuss what you have put
down with one or two others.

**rhino
behaviour** ⬅➡ **hedgehog
behaviour**

Describe typical behaviour for each family member when angry.

Name	Behaviour
_____	_____
_____	_____
_____	_____
_____	_____

For 10-week course only
Small group discussion

1. Do you tend to behave more like the rhino or the hedgehog?

_____

_____

2. What helps you to express your anger more constructively?

_____

_____

3. Do your teenagers behave more like the rhino or the hedgehog?

_____

_____

4. How could you help your teenager(s) to discuss the issue when they're angry rather than use 'passive aggressive' behaviour?

_____

_____

5. How do we make our home a safe place to express negative emotions?

_____

_____

Homework – complete **Exercise 1** on page 55–56

Part 2 Resolving conflict and handling stress

Resolving conflict

- potential for a lot of conflict over boundaries
  - teenagers want to explore; parents want to protect
  - they want to be with their friends; we want to guide them
  - they're often tired; we're often worried
- they need to see us resolving conflict effectively

Six principles for resolving conflict

1. Identify the issue

- identify the primary cause of the conflict between you
- try to find out what's going on in their lives
- easy to get annoyed about their emotional immaturity rather than addressing the underlying issue

2. Find the best time and place

- when and where are you and your teenager most likely to stay calm to discuss the issue?
- seek to have a discussion rather than a slanging match
- find enough uninterrupted time
- consider making an appointment
- ask your teenager to give you this time
- can be helpful to go out for a meal or to go for a walk

3. Discuss rather than attack

- easy to jump to conclusions
- plan carefully what you want to say
- stick to the issue
- use 'I' statements to express your feelings, *eg: 'I feel worried when ...' or 'I find it frustrating when ...'*
- listen to your teenager's point of view
- 'reflect back' what they have said (see Session 2, page 26)
- take it in turns to talk

4. Apologise, if we know we've got it wrong

- important to model apologising for our mistakes and forgiving our teenagers for theirs

5. Discuss possible solutions

- avoid getting entrenched
- involving them in a discussion is much more

productive than nagging them
- brainstorm possible solutions for the issue that's causing the conflict
- find a solution that you and your teenager can agree about
- remind them of your agreement if and when necessary

6. Remain open-minded

- stand firm on your non-negotiables
- be prepared to make compromises on other issues
- the process of discussing issues with our teenagers and looking for solutions can draw us closer to them

Handling stress

Managing our own stress

- thinking we have to be the 'perfect parent' creates anxiety and can be overwhelming
- aim to be a 'good enough parent'
- seek professional help if necessary

How to help our teenagers manage their stress

- some degree of stress is inevitable
- feeling unsupported can lead to unhealthy stress for teenagers

1. Help them learn a balance of success and failure

- let them know that mistakes and failures are a part of life – we can learn, grow and recover
- don't put unrealistic expectations onto them
- give lots of encouragement
- give praise for effort, not just for results
- tell them often you love them for who they are, not for what they achieve

2. Avoid comparing a teenager with their siblings or peers

- if they're less obviously gifted, find other characteristics to praise them for
- encourage them to be themselves
- support them in pursuing their own interests and passions

3. Create enough space for relaxation and chilling

- if necessary, cut down on extra-curricular clubs and activities
- do things just for fun
- when possible, use mealtimes, weekends and holidays for relaxation
- allow them to see us resting and relaxing

4. Talk to them about their worries

- create opportunities to talk
- some teenagers take longer to disclose their concerns and need drawing out
- allow them to voice negative feelings – anger, anxiety, fear, insecurity, a sense of failure etc

See *The Parenting Book* Section 4 for more help on handling anger and managing stress.

Small group discussion

1. Do you behave more like the 'rhino' or the 'hedgehog'? What helps you to express your anger constructively?

_____

_____

2. Do your teenager(s) behave more like the rhino or the hedgehog? How could you help your teenager(s) to discuss an issue when they're angry?

_____

_____

3. Which of the 'Six principles for resolving conflict' (see pages 50–51) stands out for you?

_____

_____

4. Can you think of a successful solution for an issue that had caused conflict, which you and your teenager(s) have come up with in the past?

_____

_____

5. How easy is it to express negative feelings in your home? What helps your teenagers to express their worries, fears and anxieties?

_____

_____

Homework – complete **Exercises 1–3** on pages 55–59

For 10-week course only
Small group discussion

1. Which of the 'Six principles for resolving conflict' (see pages 50–51) stands out for you?

_____

_____

2. What is the best time and place for you and your teenager(s) to discuss an issue that is causing conflict?

_____

_____

3. Can you think of a successful solution for an issue that had caused conflict, which you and your teenager(s) have come up with in the past?

_____

_____

4. How easy is it to express negative feelings in your home? What helps your teenagers to express their worries, fears and anxieties?

_____

_____

5. Is it safe to fail in your family?

_____

_____

Homework – complete **Exercises 2** and **3** on pages 57–59

Homework

Exercise 1

Expressing anger effectively

Identify where you want to change your own natural reactions and how you might do that.

Unhelpful reactions ✓ the ones that apply to you	Making changes ✓ the changes that you would like to make
☐ Overreacting	☐ Pressing the 'pause button', *eg: by going out of the room or counting to ten*
☐ Jumping to conclusions	☐ Hearing the whole situation before replying
☐ Shouting at our teenager	☐ Changing our tone of voice
☐ Nagging our teenager	☐ Asking our teenager to make time to sit down and discuss a situation causing conflict
☐ Keeping the peace at all costs	☐ Negotiating important boundaries
☐ Shutting our teenager down	☐ Using reflective listening for our teenager's negative thoughts and feelings
☐ Failing to impose a consequence when a boundary is crossed	☐ Having the courage to face our teenager's anger and impose a boundary
☐ Becoming cold and clinical	☐ Listening to our teenager's opinions ☐ Using 'I' statements to express our feelings, *eg:* '*I feel worried when …' or 'I find it frustrating when …'*
☐ Leaving difficult situations to the other parent	☐ Working together over boundaries and consequences
☐ Withdrawing emotionally	☐ Engaging with and drawing out our teenager's thoughts and feelings ☐ Asking open questions *ie questions that require more than a 'yes' or 'no' answer*

Please turn over ⇨

Exercise 1 (continued)

Unhelpful reactions ☑ the ones that apply to you	Making changes ☑ the changes that you would like to make
☐ Not allowing strong feelings to be expressed	☐ Encouraging appropriate expression of negative feelings, *eg: hurt, grief, disappointment, anger, embarrassment*
☐ Becoming critical of our teenager	☐ Giving our teenager daily encouragement
☐ Avoiding being together	☐ Spending time with our teenager

Identify a change you have already made:

_____

Choose three changes from the boxes you ticked and decide when you could start to make the change.

Change   **Start**

1. _____   _____

2. _____   _____

3. _____   _____

Exercise 2

Putting the six steps into practice

Use the questions below to help you think through how to resolve conflict with your teenager(s).

1. Identify the issue(s).

Write down the main issues (if any) that are currently causing conflict.

- _____

- _____

- _____

2. Find the best time and place.

When would be a good time and place to discuss one of these issues?

Time: _____

Place: _____

3. Discuss rather than attack.

What will help you to discuss the issue calmly?   _eg: take it in turns to talk_

_____

4. Apologise, if you've got it wrong.

Is there anything you need to apologise for?

_____

Please turn over

5. Discuss possible solutions.

What possible solutions have you come up with following your discussion with your teenager about one of the issues above?

- _____

- _____

- _____

Agree on one solution and see how it works – agree to review the solution in a few days/weeks time.

6. Remain open-minded.

Where have you needed to remain firm regarding that issue?

_____

Where have you made compromises in the light of your discussion?

_____

Exercise 3

Managing our teenager's stress

1. What do your children get most anxious about?

_____

How could you help them?

_____

2. Where would your teenager(s) turn if they were anxious about something?

_____

Why would they go there?

_____

3. Are there any activities your teenager(s) could drop to take off unhelpful
   pressure?

_____

_____

5

Helping Them Make
Good Choices

Review

Session 1 – Keeping the End in Mind

- helping our teenager(s) towards maturity and independence
- making our home a place of safety, of learning values for life, of fun and of learning to build relationships
- building a healthy family life through family meals, family time (having fun together) and family holidays

Session 2 – Meeting our Teenagers' Needs

- showing our teenager(s) love through (one-to-one) time, affirming words, affectionate touch, thoughtful presents and kind actions
- asking ourselves which 'love languages' make each teenager feel loved and keep their 'emotional tank' full
- remembering the importance of listening

Session 3 – Setting Boundaries

- letting them go gradually
- moving from controller to consultant
- making as few rules as possible
- being firm with important boundaries and being willing to negotiate others

Session 4 – Developing Emotional Health

- encouraging a healthy expression of anger rather than aggression (like the rhino) or suppression (like the hedgehog)
- allowing our teenager(s) to verbalise negative emotions
- giving a model for resolving conflict through discussing the issue and looking for solutions
- helping our teenager(s) to manage stress

Part 1 Giving a longer perspective

Introduction

- our task is to help equip our teenagers for the big issues they will face
- we need to talk with them about drugs, alcohol, sex, use of the Internet etc – mustn't let our fears stop us
- we can be a big influence on them, but ultimately we can't control their choices
- pressures on teenagers:
  - peer pressure
  - desire to be accepted
  - feelings of insecurity
  - relativism: 'If it feels good, then do it'
  - highly sexualised culture
  - teenagers more image-conscious today
  - accessibility of drugs, alcohol and pornography
- building their self-esteem is crucial

Passing on information and values

- we can give our teenagers a longer perspective on what is best for them and their future
- helps them to make informed choices
- enables them to construct a moral framework to live by
- we are the primary influence on our teenagers' choices – we may need to get informed ourselves

1. Drugs

- find out about the effects of drugs such as cocaine, cannabis, ecstasy on health (physical and mental) and motivation
- don't give teenagers too much money
- allow teenagers to talk generally about drugs – an indirect approach will help them to open up more than a direct accusation

2. Alcohol

- we need to recognise the values we are modelling through our own behaviour
- know about the number of units of alcohol that are considered safe for the health of adult men and women so you can have an informed discussion
- know the law and the legal age for consuming and buying alcohol
- have a 'party checklist' to talk through with your teenagers (see checklist in *The Parenting Book* Chapter 12)

3. Sex

- give teenagers permission and the confidence to say 'no'
- better to talk little and often than to have one big conversation
- look out for opportunities to talk about the proper context for sex, *eg: through discussing TV programmes, films, articles in teenage magazines, newspaper reports etc*
- need to work out our own views on pornography, abortion, sex before marriage etc, so we can talk to our teenagers about our expectations
- talk to them about the longer-term effects of STDs (sexually transmitted diseases)
- seek to give them a high view of sex

4. Internet

- online communication – talk about the opportunities and the dangers
- help them to be careful about what they post online – explain that what goes online, stays online and could potentially be seen by anybody
- limit the amount of time they spend online and/or play electronic games, so that they continue to develop their social skills
- install up-to-date filters to help protect teenagers from inappropriate content online
- the best filters, however, are our teenagers' brains if we pass on the information and values they need in order to make good choices

SMART rules for staying safe online
(to discuss with your teenager)

S   SAFE – Staying safe online involves being careful and thinking about whether it is safe to give out personal information

M   MEETING – Meeting up with someone you have contacted in cyberspace can be dangerous. Only do so with your parent's/carer's permission and when they can be present

A   ACCEPTING – Accepting e-mails or opening files from people you don't know can be dangerous – they may contain viruses or nasty messages

R   RELIABLE – Anyone can put anything on the net and remember people can lie and not be who they say they are in chat rooms

T   TELL – Tell your parent/carer or teacher if someone or something makes you feel uncomfortable or worried

Adapted from childnet.com © Copyright Childnet International 2002–2011. Reproduced with permission.

For 5- and 10-week courses
Exercise

Longer-term values

1. What are the longer-term perspectives and values you want your teenagers to take on regarding the following?

· drugs
_____

· alcohol
_____

· sex
_____

· the Internet
_____

2. What information do you need to pass on to give this longer perspective?

· drugs
_____

· alcohol
_____

· sex
_____

· the Internet
_____

Discuss what you have put down with one or two others.

For 10-week course only

Small group discussion

1. What pressures are our teenagers under in today's culture regarding drugs, alcohol, sex and the Internet?

_____

_____

2. How do we help our teenagers to construct a moral framework to live by?

_____

_____

3. What information, values and longer perspective have you tried to pass on regarding

- drugs
_____

- alcohol
_____

- sex
_____

- the Internet
_____

4. What boundaries have you put in place to help your teenagers learn about making good choices?

_____

_____

Homework – complete **Exercise 1** on pages 70–73

Part 2 Equipping our teenagers

How to help them make good choices

1. Be available to talk to them

- look for the times when they are most likely to discuss the choices they are facing

2. Rehearse scenarios

- give them language or stock lines so they have a way out when they feel under pressure
- do a role play to help them imagine the consequences of their choices

3. Give them clear explanations

- talk about dangerous situations, *eg: explain the risks of being driven by someone who has drunk alcohol*
- tell them why their behaviour can make them vulnerable to harm, *eg: help them think carefully about how they dress*

4. Ask them to keep in touch

- get them to tell you where they are and if their plans have changed

5. Encourage an active lifestyle

- helps them channel their energy constructively
- encourage them in their gifts and interests

6. Find good role models

- 'It takes a whole village to raise a child' (African proverb)
- takes some of the pressure off us as parents
- nurture relationships within the wider family
- a good youth group promoting positive values and providing friendships among their peer group can be invaluable
- try to find good role models of people in their twenties to involve in your family life

7. Create healthy traditions

- traditions and rituals help children to identify with their family and give a sense of belonging
- family traditions help create family bonds
- they make family life more fun
- they are important for passing on our values

8. Pray for them on a regular basis

- for God's protection
- for their conscience
- for their character
- praying enables us to bring our longings and our fears to God

Conclusion

- every part of this course contributes to helping our teenagers make good choices
- whatever the challenges, remember to commend positive character traits
- never give up on them. No matter what, love them unconditionally

'Love never fails.'

**1 Corinthians 13:8,
The Bible**

For 5-week course only

Small group discussion

1. What can we do to create a positive and open environment to discuss drugs, alcohol, sex, the Internet etc, with our teenagers? When have you had your best conversations?

_____

_____

2. What or who else has been most helpful to your teenagers to make good choices?

_____

_____

3. What family traditions or rituals do you have that your teenagers enjoy?

_____

_____

4. What enables you to keep going as a parent of a teenager?

_____

_____

5. What have you heard on this course that has been most helpful to you?

_____

_____

Homework – complete **Exercises 1** and **2** on pages 70–73

For 10-week course only
Small group discussion

1. What can we do to create a positive and open environment to discuss drugs, alcohol, sex, the Internet etc, with our teenagers? When have you had your best conversations?

_____

_____

2. What or who else has been most helpful to your teenagers to make good choices?

_____

_____

3. What family traditions or rituals do you have that your teenagers enjoy?

_____

_____

4. What enables you to keep going as a parent of a teenager?

_____

_____

5. What have you heard on this course that has been most helpful to you?

_____

_____

Homework – complete **Exercise 2** on page 73

Homework ✐

Exercise 1

Facing challenges

Use the following table to identify your own tendencies. Read through the different approaches and fill in the challenges you are currently facing. Then, looking back over the whole course try to work out an authoritative approach to your own challenges

Challenge	Authoritarian (harsh) approach	Indulgent/negligent approach	Authoritative (responsible) approach
Teenager not doing homework	Nag, punish, force	Bribe, do nothing, 'rescue' teen by doing it for them	Show interest. Encourage teenager to do their best. Let teen suffer consequence for not doing homework in order to learn responsibility
Teenager defies parent/ is disobedient	Threaten, force, command, overreact	Threaten, but never follow through. Plead. Resign	Postpone discussion until both calmer. Discuss situation. Impose consequence
Teenager 'forgets' chore	Get cross, nag, demand it's done immediately	Do chores yourself	Impose consequence calmly, *eg: get teenager to do one of your longer chores*
Teenager rude to parents in front of visitor	Humiliate teen in front of visitor. Make a big scene	Pretend not to notice. Plead for different behaviour	Talk about it when visitor has left. Use 'I' messages to express feelings, *eg: 'I feel embarrassed when you don't speak to our friends when they come to our home.'*
Teenager breaks a window	Lose temper, overreact, call teenager *'Careless', 'Stupid', 'Irresponsible'*	Say it doesn't matter. Sort out and pay for broken window yourself	Stay calm. Show teenager how to pick up glass safely. Make teenager pay for repair out of own money. Talk about how to avoid doing it again

Exercise 1 (continued)

Challenge	Authoritarian (harsh) approach	Indulgent/negligent approach	Authoritative (responsible) approach
Teenager hits younger sibling	Judge, blame without knowing facts, punish	Fail to notice. Console younger sibling. Ask teen not to hit	Allow siblings to settle their own fights whenever possible. Use reflective listening, *eg: 'You seem angry with your sibling.'* If necessary send to separate rooms
Teenager has been dishonest	Accuse. Shout. Put down	Excuse teenager. Find reason why it wasn't serious	Use 'I' messages to express disappointment, eg: *'I'm disappointed you ...'.* Impose consequence
Teenager gets drunk	Threaten, humiliate, treat like 4-year-old	Ignore, joke about it, fail to take action	Assist teenager to get to bed and recover. Next day make an appointment to talk through what happened
Teenager spends hours online	Not allow any time on the computer	Be content teenager is occupied and not on streets	Set time limits. Not allow until finished homework. Encourage socialising within family and with friends
Teenager wants to sleep with boyfriend/ girlfriend	Get angry, shout, accuse, humiliate	Let teenager do what s/he likes. Avoid the subject	Ask teenager for appointment to have a discussion about proper context for sex. Talk about the effects of sleeping together and then splitting up
Suspect teenager is taking drugs	Accuse teenager, refuse to let teenager go out with friends	Think drugs are too difficult a subject to tackle. Hope teenager will stop eventually	Have a discussion with teenager about the longer term effects of drug taking. Use 'Six steps for resolving conflict' to help teenager with pressure from peer group
Teenager doesn't communicate and is antisocial	Get angry, criticise teenager	Minimise any interaction. Stop having meals together	Use teenager's main love languages to build relationship. Keep having family meals

Exercise 1 (continued)

Challenge	Authoritarian (harsh) approach	Indulgent/negligent approach	Authoritative (responsible) approach
Teenager refuses to join family holiday	Insist, threaten	Give up. Let teenager go own way	Use 'Six steps for resolving conflict'
own challenge			
own challenge			
own challenge			

Adapted from Michael and Terri Quinn, *What Can a Parent Do?*

Exercise 2

Putting it into practice

What has been most helpful for you from the course that you want to remember?

1. _____

2. _____

3. _____

Appendix 1

The Parenting Teenagers Course sofa families

We are very grateful to the parents and children who agreed to appear on the DVDs and talk about their own experiences of parenting or being parented. The names in **bold** are the family members who feature.

Abi
Dayo (19) Dami (14) Timi (7)
Abi is married but is parenting alone as her husband is living abroad.

Annie and Silas
Jessie (19) Zac (18) **Mo (16)** Minnie (13) **Tallulah (13)**

Carol
David (20) **Peter (18)** Anna (16)
Carol is a single parent.

Chee-Chow and **Tim Kee**
Joel (22) **Rebekah (18)**

Con and **Madeleine**
Henry (15) **Amelia (12)** Tom (11)
Charlie (7) Johnnie (18 mths)

Dale and **Ginny**
Three adult children.

Denise and **Vincent**
Daniel (23) Matthew (21)

Elaine and Peter
Hilary (27) Patrick (24) **Emma (19)**

Eli and Jon
Noelle (15) Jocosa (2)
Eli raised Noelle as a single parent for many years. She is now married to Jon, and Jocosa is their child

Eric and **June**
Reanne (13) Sarah (11)

Helen and **Ken**
James (20) Naomi (18) Tom (16) Pip (14) Joseph (12)
Helen and Ken are parenting a 'blended' family as they both have children from former marriages.

Jo and **Tim**
Bex (15) Luke (13) Emma (12)

Karen and **Paul**
Liam (23) Christian (21) Hannah (18)

Niyi and Oyinkan
Tosin (13) Obafemi (9) Adeolu (6)

Pandora
Four adult children.
Pandora is a single parent.

Paul and **Philomena**
Patrick (16) **Emily (15) Johnnie (11) Max (10)**

Pauline and **Owen**
Yasmin (16) Rhianna (14) Daisy (10)

Simon and **Janet**
Matthew (17) Alastair (15) Dominic (12)

Steve and **Rachel**
Lauren (17) Liam (10)
Rachel is Lauren and Liam's step-mother.

Weng
Alexander (18) Oliver (16)
Weng is a single parent (with joint custody).

Appendix 2

Parenting experts

We are very grateful to the following parenting 'experts' who have generously contributed to the DVDs. Please find below contact details for them or their organisation, and some of their publications.

Harry Benson – founder of Bristol Community Family Trust; involved with family policy, research and relationship courses; author of *Let's Stick Together*: The *Relationship Book For New Parents*. **bcft.co.uk**

Lucinda Fell – Director of Policy and Communications at Childnet International, a non-profit organisation helping to make the Internet a great and safe place for children and teenagers. To access Childnet's wide range of resources to support parents and carers, see the websites **childnet.com** and **digizen.org**

Glynis Good – Couple and families relationship counsellor in Dublin, Ireland, with particular concern for supporting young people through the difficult impact of parental separation; author of *When Parents SPLIT: Support, information and encouragement for teenagers*. **whenparentssplit.com**

Timothy Johns – Headmaster, The Hawthorns School, Bletchingly, Surrey, a co-educational day school for children aged 2–13 years old

Julie Johnson – PSHE consultant and trainer; provider of parenting workshops in and around the London area, UK; child and adolescent family counsellor; Human Givens therapist; specialist in issues surrounding growing up and adolescence, bullying, loss and change, including bereavement and parental separation; author of *Being Angry* and *Bullies and Gangs* (both part of the Thoughts and Feelings series for children aged 5–10, published by Franklin Watts) and *How Do I Feel About My Stepfamily*. Julie can be contacted by email at: **julie.johnson@virgin.net**

Rob Parsons – Chairman and founder of Care for the Family; author of *The Sixty Minute Father* and *Teenagers: what every parent has to know*, among other parenting titles; international speaker on family life and business. See the Care for the Family website for further resources supporting many areas of family life. **careforthefamily.org.uk**

Dr Aric Sigman – Psychologist; biologist; broadcaster; business speaker; author of *Remotely Controlled: How television is damaging our lives*, *The Spoilt Generation: Why restoring authority will make our children and society happier* and *Alcohol Nation: How to protect our children from today's drinking culture*. **aricsigman.com**

Dr Pat Spungin – Child psychologist and family life specialist; author of *Silent Nights*, *The Haynes Teenager Manual: The practical guide for all parents*, *The Parentalk Guide to Brothers and Sisters* (co-authored with Victoria Richardson) and *Understand Your Family* (Consultant Editor). **drpatspungin.co.uk**

Appendix 3

Recommended reading

The book of the course:

The Parenting Book
by Nicky & Sila Lee (Alpha International, 2009)

Other books, alphabetical by author:

How to Really Love Your Teenager
by Ross Campbell, M.D. (Victor Books, 1993)

Anger: Handling a Powerful Emotion in a Healthy Way
by Gary Chapman (Northfield Publishing, 2007)

The Five Love Languages of Teenagers: The Secret to Loving Teens Effectively
by Gary Chapman (Northfield Publishing, 1997)

When Parents SPLIT: Support, Information and Encouragement for Teenagers
by Glynis Good (Blackhall Publishing, 2008)

What is God's Design for My Body?
by Susan Horner (Moody Publishers, 2004)

The Marriage Book
by Nicky & Sila Lee (Alpha International, 2000)

The Sixty Minute Father
by Rob Parsons (Hodder & Stoughton, 1995)

The Sixty Minute Family
by Rob Parsons (Lion, 2010)

Teenagers! What Every Parent Has to Know
by Rob Parsons (Hodder & Stoughton, 2009)

Almost Cool: You Can Figure Out How to Parent Your Teen
by Tim Smith (Moody Publishers, 1997)

New Century Version Youth Bible
(Authentic Media, 2007)

relationshipcentral.org

**If you are interested in finding out more about
The Parenting Children Course or
The Parenting Teenagers Course, where
they are running or how to start up a course,
please contact:**

Relationship Central
HTB Brompton Road
London SW7 1JA
Tel: **0845 644 7533**
Fax: **020 7589 3390**
Email: **info@relationshipcentral.org**
Website: **relationshipcentral.org**

**If you are interested in finding out more about
the Christian faith and
would like to be put in touch with your nearest
Alpha course, please contact:**

The Alpha Office
HTB Brompton Road
London SW7 1JA
Tel: **0845 644 7544**
Fax: **020 7589 3390**
Email: **ukalpha@alpha.org**
Website: **alpha.org**

Also by Nicky and Sila Lee

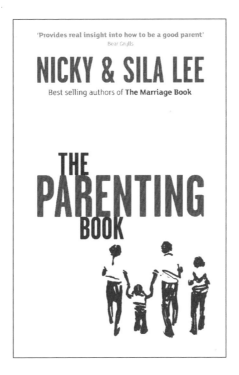

To order go to **alphashop.org**

ISBN 978 1 905887 36 1

Price £7.99

Also by Nicky and Sila Lee

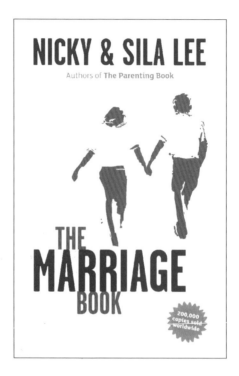

To order go to **alphashop.org**

ISBN 978 1 905887 39 2

Price £7.99